Vaughan

His Life, Work & Mission

by
Fr Robert O'Neil

*All booklets are published thanks to the
generous support of the members of the
Catholic Truth Society*

CATHOLIC TRUTH SOCIETY
PUBLISHERS TO THE HOLY SEE

Contents

Dedicated to Mr Paul Burns and Mrs Elsie Allen

Picture credits: Pages 6, 25, 38, 43, 47, 71 and 84 courtesy of Private Collection © Mill Hill Missionaries Archive Collection. Page 10: © Heritage Images / Contributor. Page 81: © Jolanta Wojcicka / Shutterstock.com

All rights reserved. First published 2017 by The Incorporated Catholic Truth Society 40-46 Harleyford Road London SE11 5AY Tel: 020 7640 0042 Fax: 020 7640 0040 © 2017 The Incorporated Catholic Truth Society.

ISBN 978 1 78469 178 3

The Shy, Gifted Communicator

True to form, our founder Herbert Vaughan renounced a considerable inheritance, a life of ease and a warm, loving family to pursue his vocation to be a priest. He had long dreamt of being a missionary to Wales. From a wealthy established Catholic family based on the Welsh borders, that had survived penal times, and the eldest of thirteen siblings, his entire life was marked by poor health. What is fascinating is that he survived at all, and greater still that he did so much.

Tall, elegant, handsome, he was by nature painfully shy, and could and did upset many by his apparent brusqueness. He was a pious and holy man, spending two hours a day in prayer, and painfully aware of his many faults. He was widely known to reconcile with enemies and to ask forgiveness of those he had offended. People knew that he spoke his mind, and with the utmost sincerity. Missionary life fascinated him from an early age – the idea of preaching the good news of the gospel. He had great devotion to St Joseph and to the Sacred Heart, and had been schooled by the Jesuits and Benedictines, and enjoyed a long association with the Carmelites. He was a man of the Victorian age, with a broad international view developed by his many travels.

Vaughan it seems was never a parish priest or even a curate, but after training in Rome became vice rector at the new seminary at Ware, during which time he investigated missionary and priestly training over many years. He co-founded a dream of Cardinal Wiseman – a missionary society of diocesan priests (Oblates of St Charles, a very revolutionary idea at the time). After widely travelling in Europe and America, investigating and fundraising (which involved much personal suffering and anxiety), at thirty-four years old he founded the Mill Hill Missionaries, a new missionary order. At forty he was made Bishop of Salford – where he remained for twenty years, visiting all his parishes, founding the Children's Rescue Society, St Bede's Commercial College for Catholic children and countless similar initiatives.

Just a few years before that he had founded The Catholic Truth Society – to become known over time as CTS Publishers and it continues to this day. It began as a small pamphleteering outfit, inspired by what Vaughan had seen of the power of the printing press in America and the disinformation he felt was being propagated there successfully by Protestant pamphleteers. He went on to buy *The Tablet* and the *Dublin Review* and was at the heart of Catholic communications for what they were in those days, since the re-establishment of the hierarchy in 1850. His working motto was essentially that the truth itself has an overwhelming attraction, and must be communicated no matter how unpopular. He was fully engaged in the hot button issues of his day, political, social and ecclesiastical – he had strong views but was ready to change or modify them where he saw the truth was better served for doing so. One of his deepest personal, spiritual crises was triggered when he was privately criticised for the speed at which he said Mass – for several years thereafter they say he often wept during Mass.

He begged to be excused his appointment as Archbishop of Westminster in 1892, at sixty, but when he could see there was no way out, he threw himself into Our Lord's hands and gave it all his energy, despite recurring and increasing illness. He was an inspiring and gifted speaker and retreat giver all his life. As a great fundraiser he raised funds to build Westminster Cathedral, surprising everyone by the sheer size of the project, its style and grandeur. The first liturgy in the almost finished cathedral was his own requiem. He died at Mill Hill on 19 June 1903, the feast of the Sacred Heart, after a long illness, aged seventy-one.

On its one hundred and fiftieth birthday, the CTS is grateful to Fr Robert O'Neil, Vaughan's biographer and a Mill Hill Missionary, to have produced such a valuable account of Vaughan's legacy of love and service.

Fergal Martin, CTS General Secretary
Feast of the Sacred Heart, June 2017

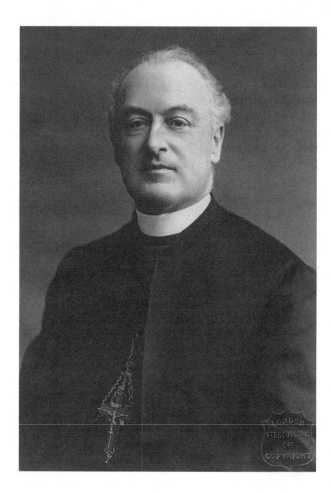

The Vaughans of Courtfield, Education, Rome and Priesthood to 1861

"Founding a missionary society would be the achievement of a lifetime for most people" but the Cardinal has "a wide ranging legacy. He shepherded the people of Salford for twenty years and fought strenuously for Catholic Education. He established the Catholic Missionary Society and the Crusade of Rescue. He started The Catholic Truth Society and the Catholic Social Union. He built Westminster Cathedral, a powerful symbol of the Catholic Church's presence at the heart of the nation."

"It is important to remember that this astonishing life of action and achievement was based on a rock-like faith. After his death, Fr Bernard Vaughan spoke of how his brother's life was 'a beautiful fusion of prayer and labour'. He spoke of how the cardinal brought all his decisions to the Lord and then 'from prayer he would arise like a giant refreshed from sleep, saying "I must be about my Father's business"!'"

Cardinal Vincent Nichols,
Message in the 2016 edition of *Cardinal Vaughan*

Herbert Alfred Vaughan was the first child of John and Louisa Elizabeth Vaughan. He was born on Sunday 15th April 1832 in Gloucester. He was born to a life of privilege on the Vaughan family estate at Courtfield on Welsh Bicknor peninsula along the River Wye.

The Vaughans of Courtfield were one of the families of the Welsh border who maintained the old faith and loyalty to Rome. The Monmouthshire area and Courtfield were regarded as a centre of recusancy, that is, those who refused to submit to the authority of the newly established Church of England.

Herbert Vaughan's grandfather William Michael Vaughan was fifteen years of age when his father died and he came into inheritance of Courtfield. He began to restore and expand the old building. He and his wife had eight children of whom three sons were ordained priests and two daughters became nuns. John Francis Vaughan, Herbert's father, was born on 2nd July 1808. He was raised at Courtfield until he was eleven years old when he was sent to the Jesuit school at Stonyhurst. There he joined the Sodality of Our Lady and began saying the little office of the Blessed Virgin, a practice he continued for the rest of his life. When he was sixteen he continued his schooling at the Jesuit school of St Achuel at Amiens in France.

According to John Snead-Cox, Herbert Vaughan's cousin and biographer, John Vaughan was very frank and energetic and a model of sincerity and directness. On

12th July 1830 John Vaughan married Louisa Elizabeth Rolls. Eliza, as she was called, was of a family of "earnest evangelicals," dissenters within the established Church of England. She was received into the Roman Catholic Church at Courtfield on 31st October 1830. Twelve years later she was confirmed by Bishop Thomas Joseph Brown.

Eliza Vaughan developed a great love for Catholic devotion and practice. To those who have read about her and her extraordinary prayer life, especially her prayer each day for one hour that her children follow a calling to the Church, she has seemed eccentric. What emerges from her correspondence is the figure of an active mother of a large family, a person with a remarkable prayer life who was at the same time filled with love and affection for her husband and children, her family and friends.

A Mother's Invocation

In a small tract which was part of the series, *The Lives of the Saints* written by John Henry Newman at Littlemore in 1844, Eliza read about Stephen Harding, one of the founders of the Cistercian order, and found a special inspiration. "Ever since I read the account of St Bernard and his four brothers leaving the world and retiring to a monastery I have prayed that all my sons will follow their example." She was confident her fourteen year old son "Herbert will become a priest."

Each day for nearly twenty years Eliza Vaughan spent an hour between 5 and 6 p.m. at prayer before the Blessed Sacrament in the manor house chapel. At some point she began to add the prayer of Elizabeth, the mother of Bernard of Clairvaux, that some of her children would be called to serve God. In answer to her prayer, all of her five daughters became nuns and six of her eight sons became priests.

Herbert Vaughan's mother, Eliza Rolls Vaughan.

Herbert Vaughan kept by him, until shortly before his death in 1903, a tiny picture of his mother. About her his brother Bernard once said "Herbert was unable to speak without emotion." John Vaughan thought that his son Herbert would become his successor and squire of Courtfield. Perhaps he would pursue an army career. Herbert's mother hoped that God had other plans for her son who often watched her from the gravel path in the garden praying before the Blessed Sacrament in the house chapel.

Herbert's first formal schooling took place at St Mary's Mission in Monmouth. The mission church was a small, plain meeting house hidden behind homes on St Mary's Street. A school had been opened in 1836 and a few years later Mr Vaughan brought his sons Herbert and Roger to be students. The teacher was Thomas Burgess Abbot, nephew of the parish priest.

Herbert left Monmouth in 1841 and was enrolled at the Jesuit School, Stonyhurst. His studies began at Stonyhurst Preparatory School, Hodder Place, in Birmingham. He was almost nine years old. Like his father before him, Herbert became a member of the Sodality of Our Lady. Almost sixty years later, he wrote: "I was solemnly consecrated to our Blessed Lady when I was thirteen years of age." He was very young entering Stonyhurst and left when he was only fourteen when he enrolled at another Jesuit school at Brugelette in Belgium. At the Belgium school there was an enrolment of three hundred boys. He studied there for three years. While he was at home in Courtfield in 1848 he went on a retreat where he decided to become a priest and devote his life to the Welsh mission.

News of Herbert's intention was a great disappointment to his father. At the end of his life John Vaughan wrote that he had hoped Herbert would have a good career as a soldier and succeed him at Courtfield. Yet he was too good to oppose such a vocation and said simply: "Well, if Herbert goes, all the others may go too," which they all nearly did.

Herbert proposed to his father and Bishop Thomas Joseph Brown, OSB, vicar apostolic of the Welsh-speaking district, that he go to Brecon and learn the language under a Welsh-speaking priest in preparation to become a missionary in Wales. The bishop did not agree to this plan, but Herbert did not abandon the idea to become a missionary. He was probably influenced not only by his heritage as a Vaughan, but also by a revival that was taking place at that time which seemed to make a return to the old faith in Wales a possibility.

"Making More Elbow Room"

In the summer of 1850 Herbert entered St Gregory's, Downside, the Benedictine school near Bath. He had not gone to Downside to become a Benedictine but to join the young monks who were studying theology. He lived with the monastic community and dressed just as those studying at seminaries in Ushaw and Oscott.

A battle with poor health troubled Herbert Vaughan throughout his life. When he took an army physical it became clear that his health was not as good as his appearance led others to believe. Heart problems were not unknown to the family; his brother Roger had been withdrawn from school because of a suspected weak heart. At Downside the students learned that the eighteen year old Herbert Vaughan, though "of splendid athletic build...had a weak heart." Years later a former student remembered him as a young man with a strong personality, forceful and earnest, and, although naturally reserved, helpful to others.

At some point Vaughan went to Fr Placid Hall about becoming a Benedictine monk and was told "Young man!

You will want more elbow room than you would find here." A final comment written in a letter to the *Downside Review* said that "Cardinal Vaughan's life's work was finding or making of more elbow room."

In the summer of 1851 Herbert Vaughan left Downside to begin his studies for the secular priesthood in Rome. His mother wrote in her missal: "Our beloved child Herbert left us on Monday 13th October 1851 and crossed to Boulogne on his way to the eternal city on 23rd October."

Herbert Vaughan left England with his cousin, William Clifford – who became Bishop of Clifton in 1857 – and a Mr Maskell, a convert and former chaplain to the Anglican Bishop of Exeter. They travelled in stages by horse-drawn coach finally reaching Rome on 15th November 1851. In Rome he began at once to enquire about attending lectures at the Collegio Romano. In his diary he wrote about the hopes he had for a mission to Wales.

The student Vaughan was described as tall and fair, stern with "fearless blue eyes, aquiline nose and firm set mouth." In temperament, he was impulsive, warm-hearted and humble, and, despite the austerities he practised throughout his life, along with a piercing sense of his personal unworthiness, he had an excellent sense of humour.

On his return from a visit home in the summer of 1852 he travelled with Henry Edward Manning, who he was to succeed years later as Archbishop of Westminster. As a travelling companion he was impatient with Manning whom he referred to as a "grave and solemn convert parson." While in Rome Vaughan lived at Pontifical Academy, a house for the sons of aristocrats, while attending the Roman College. The College was a Jesuit school and forerunner of the Gregorian University.

A Great Sadness

On 2nd January 1853 Vaughan visited Church historian Dr Daniel Rock. He brought up his idea again about a mission to Wales which included a seminary in Rome to train missionaries. Rock encouraged Vaughan's ideas. He wrote in his diary that a seminary for Wales became his "uppermost thought."

There were many English in Rome at the time. An Italian told him that "wherever you go you are sure to see English from the top of St Peter's to the least interesting sight." But despite all the activity and energy seen in the pages of his diary his health was not going well. So seriously did it deteriorate at the beginning of 1853 – probably due to the effects of heart disease – that others became convinced that he might not live to the age required for Holy Orders. His body was betraying him and this led to difficulties with the self-discipline of student life and contributed to his depression and introspection, as seen in his diary entries.

At the beginning of February 1853 a great sadness entered Vaughan's life when news reached him from Courtfield that his mother had died. It was a storm which brought an end to the happiness of the Vaughans at Courtfield. Mrs Vaughan was preparing to deliver her fourteenth child. She was only forty two years old. When a son, John, was born in January 1853, and she lost her life, her youngest daughter, Margaret, was only seventeen months old.

Herbert wrote once that he often thought of his mother and talking "to her now and I am sure she hears me; she answers me in whispers and spreads over my soul a great calm. I invoke her as a saint; whenever I call upon one Mother, I call upon the other."

At the beginning of 1854 Vaughan was so ill that his friends thought he was going to die. In April he left Rome hoping to recover his health and ended up with his uncle Thomas Weld-Blundell near Florence. The Vatican was petitioned to allow for his ordination eighteen months earlier than is ruled in Canon Law. He left for a Passionist monastery in Lucca in September 1854 and was ordained to the priesthood at a Franciscan convent in Bargo, near Lucca on Saturday 28th October 1854. And so Herbert Vaughan's priesthood began quietly with his ordination and, two days later, a first Mass witnessed by a few well-wishers. Afterwards he wandered in the Italian hills with only the company of his thoughts, one of which concerned a request from Nicholas Wiseman. Wiseman had written a letter to offer Vaughan the vice-presidency of St Edmund's College, Old Hall Green, Ware, in Hertfordshire.

It is not known what moved the cardinal to appoint such a young and inexperienced man to be vice-president at Old Hall Green, but an acquaintance of Vaughan, Robert Whitty, Wiseman's vicar-general may have had something to do with Herbert Vaughan's acceptance of the post.

Ultramontanism

St Edmund's College is near to the village of Old Hall Green, about five miles from Ware, in Hertfordshire. Lay students and seminarians made up the student body. In the 1850s it was the seminary of the two dioceses which at that time covered the whole south of England. It was one of Wiseman's priorities on the restoration of the hierarchy in England to improve the training of the seminarians at St Edmund's College.

Nicholas Wiseman, along with Henry Edward Manning, helped to determine the path of Herbert Vaughan's career in the Church. Although he was thoroughly English in his sympathies and habits, Wiseman's main qualification was that he had been completely "Romanised", between 1818 and 1840, by his experience as a student and rector of the English College in Rome. Wiseman viewed Rome as the centre not only of the Church but also of all their religious ideals. His views were opposed by "Old Catholics" and even his own chapter. The movement that worked to centralise all authority under the Bishop of Rome was labelled "Ultramontanism." These problems underlay the difficulties Vaughan was to encounter at St Edmund's between 1855 and 1861.

It was the convert, Henry Edward Manning, who Wiseman used in his efforts to Romanise the Church. And it was Manning, although twenty four years older than Vaughan, who was to treat the younger man like his own son. Edward Norman compared the two men. Between them there was a difference of background and temperament. Vaughan was raised in the world of the Catholic gentry while Manning's world was of the establishment with its links to Harrow and Oxford. Vaughan was "retiring by nature whereas Manning became so only after his wife's death." Another thought Vaughan had a vigorous mind, "neither complex nor original, but clear." Manning was already mature and confident due to his connections and education. He was also a "thinker and pietist" while Vaughan was an activist. What they did have in common during their long and sometimes shaky friendship was a "developed interior life."

One of Cardinal Wiseman's first acts to reform St Edmund's was to appoint a convert, William George Ward, as lecturer in moral philosophy. He and his wife were to become lifelong friends and benefactors of Herbert Vaughan.

Oblates of St Charles

Wiseman had another idea to help reform the clergy of his diocese. It led to the formation of the Oblates of St

Charles. Manning drew up a rule using the model of a sixteenth century congregation of Oblates founded by Charles Borromeo in Milan. When Vaughan went to St Edmunds he also offered to join Manning's Oblates. As Herbert Vaughan did throughout his career he prepared very well. In this case he studied and visited some of the principal seminaries of Europe. Before he was thirty, he was to be one of the best-informed men of his time on the training and state of the secular clergy.

In 1855 Herbert Vaughan arrived at St Edmund's full of enthusiasm and ideas collected on his travels. He had given up his idea of becoming a missionary in Wales in favour of Wiseman's plan to prepare apostolic priests for the conversion of England. And yet, he did not completely abandon his thoughts of a life as a missionary.

The presence of Vaughan at the College and the Oblates in the archdiocese was opposed by others especially the majority of Wiseman's own chapter. As a community of secular priests, the Oblates were seen as unlawful intruders in the diocese who aimed at taking control of the seminary at Old Hall Green. In the spring of 1860 Vaughan was sick again with suspected smallpox. When he returned to school in the autumn of 1860 the situation of he and other Oblates at St Edmund's remained stormy. The Oblates finally left St Edmund's in the summer of 1861. At the time it was considered by some to be "the most notorious English Catholic dispute of the century."

Disappointed and frustrated by the circumstances surrounding his tenure at St Edmund's, and finally by Rome's order to withdraw the Oblates, Herbert Vaughan began to dream again of a great adventure: "In proportion as I saw I could do nothing at St Edmund's in the direction I wished, the idea of foreign missions grew upon me."

Herbert Vaughan and the Missionary College at Mill Hill to 1872

> His frequent visits were the great excitement of our early youth…Every time he visited us he told us of some exciting scheme of his own for the glory of the Church, and we were profoundly interested in his plan of going to America in order to collect money for the founding of a college for foreign missions. He was to start at the end of 1863, but before he went he brought to fulfilment the consecration of my eldest sister to the religious life…
>
> Maisie Ward, *The Wilfred Wards and the Transition*

"I am most willing and glad that you should use all the efforts in your power to collect means for beginning such a work and that when begun you should devote yourself to it." Henry Edward Manning, 20th June 1863.

Herbert Vaughan was never completely free from the "haunting wish to get away from civilisation altogether, and in some far land devote himself, body and soul, to the work of converting the heathen." According to his cousin John Snead-Cox, the wish to become a missionary remained at the back of his mind during his days at Rome and later at St Edmund's. It was something he had to resolve.

Vaughan's enthusiasm for the foreign missions remained throughout his life. He came to be respected internationally as a promoter of the missionary work of the Church. In his final days, he explained his understanding of the Church's mission and the standards expected of a missionary, in a collection of conferences on the apostolic life entitled *The Young Priest*.

Herbert Vaughan tried to enlist the help of others in his commitments to the foreign missions; not everyone shared his, at times, impulsive enthusiasms. More than one commentator agreed that for Herbert Vaughan evangelisation was the hallmark of true Christianity. Even at Salford where he was to be bishop for twenty years he was regarded by a historian of the diocese as "essentially a missionary bishop" who treated his diocese as a "small mission field."

Among his many accomplishments, the most romantic, and one of the greatest achievements of Herbert Vaughan's life, was the founding of a missionary college in the north west London suburb of Mill Hill. Vaughan's foundation, the first of its kind in the Catholic Church in England, was to inspire "generations of Catholic young men with noble vocations to wider service."

At first Vaughan thought of being a missionary to Australia following the example of Bishop Ullathorne. Then he returned to his dream of being a missionary in Wales. But his travels in Europe and his studies had broadened his interests.

An Opportunity for Evangelisation

At home Vaughan also had the example of ambitious Protestant missionary movements such as the Society for the Propagation of Christian Knowledge and the Society for the Propagation of the Gospel and later the Church Missionary Society and the British and Foreign Bible Society. The achievement of the Protestants proved to be an incentive for a Catholic foreign missionary effort, not only in England, but in the United States. Herbert Vaughan also knew about the work of Catholic missionaries and missionary groups on the Continent and in Ireland. He sought the advice of Henry Edward Manning who gave him his slender encouragement saying that something may come of Vaughan's dreams.

In the spring and summer of 1860 Vaughan continued to collect information about seminary training and missionary – sending organisations. He pursued his idea for another two years in spite of "a torment of doubts." In May 1860 he visited All Hallows College in Dublin founded by Fr John Hand. Vaughan continued to search for a model. In June he went to France and then Italy. Throughout this period Vaughan used his skills as a keen observer and drew on the experience of many others to formulate a plan of his own. Like others before him he saw an opportunity for evangelisation laid open by an expanding British Empire. His diaries reflect his uncertainty but also his single-mindedness to search for a model to follow in England.

He spoke to Cardinal Wiseman about his thoughts and discovered that Wiseman had had a conversation with Vincent Pallotti in Rome soon after Wiseman had become a bishop. Pallotti, who had founded a missionary society, told Wiseman that he would never find the rest he wanted until he had established a "College in England for the Foreign Missions." Afterwards Cardinal Wiseman was not able to see a way to keep to Pallotti's prediction and decided to wait for someone who would take up the task. Vaughan became that person, but not at once.

At first it was proposed to add the training of candidates for the foreign missions to be part of a plan for an Oblate novitiate and seminary. The proposal was rejected.

Perfect Trust in God

In the beginning of 1863 Vaughan was ill again and Wiseman sent him to Spain for a complete rest. He continued to think about a missionary seminary and sought the advice of others, first in Barcelona and then in Seville. In Seville during March he prayed to St Joseph and consulted with the Jesuit, Joaquin Medina. Medina advised him not to worry about his poor health saying that God "could use us for his purposes without such health." Vaughan concluded soon after that he must make a start in a rented house.

On 20th April during his Mass he had the inspiration to begin quietly at Bayswater, renting rooms, and go to

South America to beg for financial support. Yet Vaughan continued to suspect that he was dreaming and deceiving himself about such a project. He went on retreat at the beginning of May at El Puerto de la Santa Maria. The director, Victorio Medrano, was a native of St Francis Xavier's home in Navarre. Medrano advised Vaughan to begin his project humbly and have perfect trust in God. "We must often begin good works and bear to see them come to an end." To always try. Thanks to Joaquin Medina and the practical Victorio Medrano, Herbert Vaughan's mind was settled. Snead-Cox concluded: "In such tribulation of soul was born the Missionary Society of Mill Hill."

On return to England Cardinal Wiseman invited Vaughan to address a meeting of bishops in July 1863. All but one bishop gave approval of his proposal but they promised no material support for the foreign missions.

He prepared for a begging trip to the Americas. As throughout his life his preparations were thorough and energetic. He prayed, sought advice and approval, and then laid the foundations for the undertaking. Once he had completed his preparations, he went ahead, with no evidence of his former hesitation and self-doubt. He always worked hard and prepared well. He was a dreamer, an adventurer and a romantic, but in addition to these traits, he had a practical approach to challenges and an ability to persevere.

St Joseph's College, Mill Hill.

"An Inexpressible Confidence"

In October 1863 Vaughan travelled to Rome where Pope
Pius IX gave his blessing. He returned to England and
prepared to leave from Southampton on 17th December
1863. The day before he left Wiseman wrote to him that
he felt "an inexpressible confidence...God...will prosper
this work, such as I have never...felt in any other."

All signs of depression and self-doubt seem to have
disappeared as he went aboard the steamer, the *SS Taranto*.
With his assortment of letters from the Pope, Propaganda,
Cardinal Wiseman, and from bishops, diplomats and
friends, he began his journey arriving fourteen days
later on 31st December 1863 in St Thomas, the Virgin
Islands. By January, he was on the coast of Nicaragua
before getting to Panama. Crossing the isthmus by train
he found an American steamer, the *Saint Louis*, and left
for California. With over three hundred passengers the
journey took seventeen days to San Francisco.

He began his journey with two small notebooks. One
had the names and addresses for introductions on his trip
and the other was titled "Education Fund." The first entry
for January 1864 in Panama was "Felix Clausel, 20 New
Grenadian dollars." He went to see the archbishop and was
disappointed when told he would not have permission to
collect money in his diocese, an area the size of France. He
made a concession: one appeal in a country area.

Vaughan set off for Marysville and Bishop Eugene O'Connell, a former dean of All Hallows in Dublin. O'Connell gave him permission to preach as much as he wished. At the end of March the Archbishop of San Francisco had a change of heart and gave his permission to preach wherever he wished in his diocese. Vaughan remained five months in California and his time there remained a happy memory until the end of his life.

It was there he met a Belgian missionary to Native Americans in Oregon who advised that missionaries needed to be part of a congregation with a centre. From their conversation an idea began to take shape that it was not enough to have a missionary training seminary and from that idea developed St Joseph's Society for Foreign Missions.

Training Missionaries

On 23rd June Vaughan sailed for South America, making stops along the way, before arriving at Lima, Peru on 18th July. When he arrived in Peru, the Church and bishops were paralysed by an anti-religious government. He was forbidden by the government to collect money there. The proclamation had no effect. On a visit to the President his wife gave him a donation of two hundred and fifty dollars. He left Peru for Chile and finally arrived in Santiago after an overland journey from Valparaíso on about 19th

October. At the end of February he left by ship around the Cape for Rio de Janeiro arriving on 4th April.

It was at Rio he learned that Cardinal Wiseman had died on 15th February. The Emperor and Empress of Brazil became patrons of his project and the Empress gave him one thousand dollars. As more money was donated he became confident that he should begin a seminary on his own, separate from the Oblates. By that time he had collected about ten thousand pounds and had promises of more to come later.

Back in England Manning had been named Wiseman's successor. Manning instructed Vaughan to return to England at once. Alone with his thoughts as he crossed the Atlantic, he refined his ideas about a missionary college and a congregation of missionaries. It was not to follow the model of Ireland's All Hallows, but to be similar to those of the Continent, especially that of the Paris Foreign Missions Society of Rue du Bac. When the mail boat reached Bordeaux, Vaughan travelled first to Paris, where he prayed at Notre Dame des Victoires, and then went on to England. It was the last week of July 1865.

Edward Norman considers the foundation by Herbert Vaughan of a college to train missionaries for work overseas to be one of the greatest achievements of his life. With funds and experience from his travels to North and South America, Vaughan was about to make his years of planning and hard work a reality.

Henry Edward Manning, now the new Archbishop of Westminster, encouraged Vaughan to devote all his energy to beginning a missionary college. His friends from St Edmund's Mr and Mrs William George Ward gave him a gift of two thousand pounds and undertook to help him find a suitable place to start. At the same time he began to look for candidates. He visited the Redemptorists and Marists in Ireland. In 1866 the Redemptorists directed to Vaughan the first candidate to be ordained from his future college, a young man named Cornelius Dowling, a native of Fermoy.

Devotion to St Joseph

Mrs Ward found a place to begin, Holcombe House in Mill Hill, a rural area about eleven miles from the centre of London. At the time Holcombe House was leased to a Baker Street businessman named Charles Thomas Druce. Druce was not interested in transferring the lease. Vaughan put the challenge into the hands of his trusted friend St Joseph. More than once during his life, Vaughan showed a simple and unshakeable confidence in St Joseph. Vaughan wrapped a small statue of St Joseph and left it at the Bruce home saying that he would pick up the parcel later. On the last day of a novena to St Joseph the agent for the Bruce family wrote that they were willing to transfer the leasehold. In the end Vaughan decided to buy the freehold of the property from the owner.

Before moving to Holcombe House, Vaughan published an address to the Catholics in England on the Feast of the Martyrs of Japan, on 5th February 1866, looking for popular support for a College for the Foreign Missions. He urged more sacrifice and held to the belief that the sending out of missionaries was a sign of a mature Christianity and would be rewarded at home – the gospel paradox that the one who gives will receive.

The object of the College was to educate secular priests for foreign missions beyond the seas. Youths of every nation would be admitted but it should be kept in mind that the College was only provisional and introductory, and the aim was to provide "a good native clergy" everywhere. A foreign missionary college, he wrote, "is to work towards its own extinction."

On 28th February 1866 Vaughan, along with another Oblate, Henry Bayley, and the first student, Henry Osmond, left Bayswater for Mill Hill. The next morning, 1st March 1865, the first Mass was celebrated at Holcombe House. On 17th March the sale of the house and property was complete. Vaughan paid £5,397 12 s 4 d. On Monday 19th March the feast of St Joseph, Mass was celebrated. Manning was present and declared the College begun.

Throughout his career Vaughan was a keen observer who prepared well for his projects as he did at Mill Hill. Although his views changed as the foundation grew, in the beginning he was quite uncompromising in his frugality.

Dependence on God

Sometime in 1866 a woman who was to become the foremost benefactor of Vaughan's seminary, and known as "Mother of the Mill" for her kindnesses to the foundation, visited Holcombe House. She was Mary Elizabeth Herbert, a convert and widow of Sidney Herbert, Lord Herbert of Lea, who had been directed to Holcombe House by Henry Edward Manning. She was one of the notable women of the Victorian era and a friend of W E Gladstone and Florence Nightingale. Not only was she to become one of the founders of the Foreign Missionary College at Mill Hill but also of an orphanage for girls at Salisbury. She wrote numerous books and pamphlets over her lifetime and was the mother of the thirteenth and fourteenth Earls of Pembroke.

When her husband died in 1861 she was left with seven children, four boys and three girls. Largely due to the influence of Henry Edward Manning she was received into the Catholic Church. She had been married about four months when she first met Manning, who was then an Anglican. "My husband one day brought to introduce to me one whom he called his oldest school and college friend," she wrote.

She was received into the Catholic Church on 5th January 1865 in the archbishop's private chapel in the cathedral at Palermo, Sicily. Becoming a Catholic caused her great sorrow in her family life. And yet a grand-daughter remembered that after many disappointments and sorrows in her life she had learned "a dependence on God, and a strength which never forsook her."

After she became a Catholic she travelled from Wilton to London to go to confession to Archbishop Manning who then lived at York Place in London. One day as she was leaving, Manning said to her "I want you to go down and see Herbert Vaughan's new little house at Mill Hill where he is beginning his Foreign Missionary work. I confess I do not know how he will succeed but it was a favourite idea of Cardinal Wiseman, and he himself is full of faith and energy about the undertaking."

"Our Duty to the Heathen"

Vaughan travelled to Rome in the winter of 1866-7. At Genoa he fell seriously ill from a leg wound that had become infected.

Over the next two years he travelled and made contact with missionary institutions that he hoped might take on the running of the missionary college. He did not receive the help he hoped for from his Oblate community. One reason was they were over-taxed by a new house of studies in Rome.

His seminary was not modelled on Ireland's All Hallows because it prepared priests for the Irish diaspora. His aim was to prepare missionaries for "pagan" areas of the world in Asia and sub-Saharan Africa. This would involve primary evangelisation and care by the seminary for the people it sent out. He hoped for help from the Paris Foreign Mission. He was unsuccessful. He tried the Vincentians and also failed.

In February 1869 he was despondent about what he considered a poor beginning for his missionary college. He tried with the Holy Ghost Fathers in France and failed again. It became clear that he must devote himself to running the college.

From 1866 Vaughan was rector of the missionary college at Mill Hill but he soon became involved with the work of Archbishop Manning and in 1868 with ownership of the Catholic weekly *The Tablet*.

Henry Edward Manning confided in Vaughan on matters concerning the English Catholic Church and Vaughan in turn acted on the archbishop's behalf. One of the tasks that Manning gave Vaughan was to be pro-vicar general for the religious convents in the archdiocese. One was a group of Anglican nuns who worked in Hackney. They had written to Lady Herbert asking if she had ever regretted becoming a Catholic. Manning prepared to receive the community into the Catholic Church. They later bought Holcombe House when a new college was built and founded, St Mary's Abbey, Mill Hill.

Manning organised a great meeting at St James's Hall, Piccadilly, on 24th April 1868. He reminded the audience that as members of the British Empire and English speakers they had a special duty to spread the faith that others did not have. Vaughan spoke and presented a plan to build a permanent missionary college for six thousand pounds. The name chosen was to be St Joseph's College of the Sacred Heart for Foreign Missions. The meeting passed resolutions in support of the College. A pamphlet was published, prepared by Vaughan and titled "Our Duty to the Heathen." A supporting organisation was formed called St Joseph's Society of the Sacred Heart for Foreign Missions. The secretary was Mr E G Shapscote of York Place in London. There was such a good response that Vaughan prepared to lay the foundation stone of St Joseph's College in June 1869.

Purchasing *The Tablet*

Herbert Vaughan purchased *The Tablet* in the summer of 1868. The Catholic press in the nineteenth century was combative and partisan. *The Tablet* was no exception. Unlike so many other newspapers of the nineteenth century it has survived.

Vaughan bought it for nine hundred pounds. His cousin Snead-Cox thought it "was the luckiest investment of his life." However Vaughan's inexperience and temperament, especially his bluntness, did not endear him to readers. In addition Vaughan did not have the literary gifts of a Ward or Manning. This did not mean he was an ineffective communicator. The editor of *The Month* wrote an appreciation of Vaughan long after his death, in 1910.

He stressed that if the excellence of a good style is based on unpretentiousness, simplicity, directness, lucidity and force, his had these qualities. He quickly seized with an intelligent grasp the points of a subject, intellectual and practical, when it was brought to his notice.

The main reason Vaughan bought *The Tablet* was his appreciation of the Catholic press. During his trip to the United States in 1865 he had been impressed by the influence of newspapers. He was a friend of Isaac Hecker, the founder of the Paulists, a man who was convinced of the importance of the apostolate of the press and founded the *Catholic World*. His friendship with Ward, of the *Dublin Review*, and the experience of his father when he studied in Paris also influenced him.

Once Vaughan hired an editor who was eventually his cousin John Snead-Cox, and freed from the stress of deadlines, the abrasiveness that characterised his *Tablet* writing disappeared from his other activities. It was not until Vaughan became Bishop of Salford in 1872 that he had a chance to mature into "the noble character he was in the last and greatest phase of his life."

The Founding of CTS

Remarkably, Vaughan had time for other ventures while he was publishing *The Tablet*, caring for his missionary college, and travelling the Continent and the United States. For example, in 1868 he founded The Catholic

Truth Society. The idea to produce inexpensive pamphlets about the Catholic Faith was not new; the first pamphlets originated at least as far back as 1829, the year of Catholic Emancipation. In 1832 there was a Catholic society for the distribution of prayer books and other material, and in 1834 the Catholic Tract Society, followed by the Catholic Institute in 1838. In 1868 Vaughan revived the idea and presented a model that he learned of in the United States in *The Tablet*. The aims were twofold: "to instruct Catholics in their faith" and to dissipate "popular prejudice and error among non-Catholics." He was helped by Lady Herbert of Lea and Fr George Bampfield, a convert. The Catholic Truth Society offices were in London and in 1869 a branch was opened in Manchester. But the Society failed in 1870 only to be revived in 1884 through the efforts of James Britten. Britten's new society had branches overseas within the next four years. Vaughan gave all the stock he had from the earlier attempt and became the CTS president. He once said in 1868: "We are in the age of the Press. It can penetrate where no Catholic can enter...It is an instrument in our hands."

First Missionary Colleges

After three years at Holcombe House in Mill Hill Vaughan went ahead to construct a new college on an adjacent property. A partially finished St Joseph's College was opened, free from debt, on 1st March 1871. There were thirty four students. The first missionary priest, Cornelius Dowling from Fermoy, Cork, Ireland, had been ordained on 27th December 1869. Elizabeth Herbert gave the College two paintings, one of St Joseph and the other of the Sacred Heart, both central to Vaughan's devotional life. The cornerstone for a memorial chapel in honour of St Joseph was laid on 19th March 1871.

During this time Vaughan worked on the legal status of the College in the Church and the placement of his ordained missionaries. He was in Rome in 1870 waiting for approval of the "Fundamental Rules and Oath" that would bind his missionaries together and a mission assignment. He returned to London empty handed but unknown to him a search was underway for missionaries to work in the United States among African-Americans. An appeal reached him from Bishop Spalding in Baltimore. In the autumn of 1871 the Pope assigned Vaughan's first four priests to America to "evangelise Negroes" and granted the small band the title of "apostolic missionaries" with Herbert Vaughan as the superior of the St Joseph's Society of the Sacred Heart. Herbert Vaughan and his four missionaries were welcomed by Spalding in Baltimore on 5th December 1871. They made their home at St Francis Xavier Church in Baltimore. Vaughan's vision was not only to work among African-Americans but to found a missionary college in the United States which might train African-Americans to return as missionaries to Africa.

After settling his small band Vaughan began a tour of the Post-Civil War United States, especially to areas where his missionaries might be called upon to work. What he saw of the treatment of African-Americans by white Catholics shocked him. He had not realised the "intensity" of the dislike by white Americans. Wherever he went he asked about the experience of Protestant-sponsored missions. For example he wrote in his diary, "Why cannot we have catechists of brothers like the Methodist preachers"?

In New York he stayed at St Paul's Church on Ninth Avenue with his friend Isaac Hecker, the founder of the

With the first missionaries in Baltimore, USA.

Paulists. Wherever he could he collected money for the new mission. By 1st May he had collected twelve thousand dollars. One result of his visit was the recruitment of John Slattery who was a New Yorker and as a Mill Hill Missionary later became a supporter of African-Americans. One wrote that at the end of the nineteenth century the cause of black priests in the Catholic Church had no greater champion than the Reverend John R Slattery. There were other recruits at Mill Hill when he arrived there. Slattery wrote that when he studied at Mill Hill there were seven American students.

There was a serious setback to the mission when Cornelius Dowling died a victim of typhoid fever in August. Over the next six years, administrative and philosophical difficulties, combined with a lack of manpower and money, nearly destroyed the American mission.

Vaughan returned to England after a seven month absence in 1872. By September there were ninety students and staff at St Joseph's College. On 29th September he learned that Rome had chosen him to be the Bishop of Salford.

Vaughan's enthusiasms and personal style, seen in the founding of the missionary college at Mill Hill and the introduction of the first missionaries to the United States, were special. The weakness of his effort was that he was soon drawn away and his missionaries were left with few guidelines. His practical genius lay in his personal involvement and hands-on approach to his projects, but his energy and active mind constantly pulled him away, so that it was humanly impossible to always apply his strengths effectively. The Salford appointment had the same result; he was drawn away from his missionary college while remaining its head and administrator from his new diocese in Lancashire.

Bishop of Salford 1872

"Our founder, Cardinal Vaughan, was inspired by a vision (at Salford) whereby the pursuit of educational excellence in the last quarter of the nineteenth century was open to the Catholic children of Manchester." John Byrne, Headmaster of St Bede's, in the *Universe*.

> Herbert Vaughan spent twenty years at Salford. Yet the record of Salford is brief about his good works and silent about his relationship with other community leaders. For example…his Church of England counterpart for many of those years, James Fraser…He and Vaughan shared a great affection for Lancashire, and Fraser, like Vaughan, was also well known for his hard work, thrift and straightforward manner…In 1879 Fraser wrote to a friend that Vaughan was an "able and accomplished man," and whenever they met on neutral grounds, they always met as friends.
>
> *Cardinal Vaughan*, 2016 edition, p 521

Vaughan's appointment to Salford was controversial. One reason was that he was virtually unknown to the Catholic Church in the North of England, with its line of St Cuthbert's Seminary and Stonyhurst College ecclesiastics. But Cardinal Manning succeeded in moving him forward and Vaughan spent twenty years as bishop in Lancashire. Salford was geographically small but otherwise one of the most important dioceses in England, comprising Manchester and the industrial centres of the north west.

When Vaughan came in 1872 there were about one hundred thousand Catholics in the whole diocese, mostly working class and urban, their number swelled by the immigration of Irish Catholics. Charles Bolton, in his history of the diocese, records Vaughan's tenure: recruiting clergy on the Continent, especially in Holland, establishing a Pastoral Seminary, St Bede's College, The Catholic Rescue Society, The Catholic Truth Society and more than forty new parishes among other works. In 1892 when Vaughan was appointed to Westminster he wrote: "It would have been hard for any man to assume the mantle of Bishop Vaughan."

Wiseman, Manning and Vaughan guided the re-established Church away from the insularity of "Old Catholics" and made it part of the international Catholic institutional community.

After he surveyed Salford diocese he decided on a number of projects. One was to make the administration of the diocese more business-like. He organised annual synods and increased the responsibilities of deans. Finances were centralised and a board appointed to advise him on financial matters. Personally he planned to model his life on that of Charles Borromeo who made his palace like a monastery. Throughout his life he refused to go into

Herbert Vaughan, Bishop of Salford, 1872-1892.

debt and simply pay off the interest. He always tried to pay off the principal. It became a practice to use fifteen percent or twenty percent of the parish collections for building improvements to reduce parish debt. His efforts did not make him universally popular with his priests.

One project he initiated at Salford was to establish a pastoral seminary for the education of the diocesan clergy who came from all parts of Europe. He wrote that his priests were known for their zeal and now he wanted that they be "pre-eminent for their learning." He decided to establish a seminary of pastoral theology attached to the cathedral. After their third year of theology at one of the country's major seminaries they would spend a year in the pastoral seminary continuing their studies and learning the practical tasks of being a priest in a parish. The classes began in 1874 and over the five years of its existence sixty five priests passed through its doors.

St Bede's Commercial College

At Salford Vaughan entered into a dispute with the Jesuits over schools and education in the diocese. There was a fundamental question at stake: what was the authority of a bishop in his diocese? It was also a struggle for influence over the growing middle-class Catholic community in the nineteenth century and an effort to raise the status of the secular clergy. After many trips to Rome, and an absence for a year-and-a-half between 1879 and 1881, Rome favoured the bishops with a decision known as *Romanos Pontfices*. This proclamation did not end the dispute between bishops and religious orders but it was seen to strengthen the authority of the bishops in their dioceses.

A joke went around that whenever Herbert Vaughan had five spare minutes, he would call his secretary and ask what new project he could start. One major project was the founding of St Bede's Commercial College. He lived at the College in a room attached to the school. For fourteen of his twenty years at Salford he lived there simply and shared life with the staff and students. The practice was for students to live with "superiors as far as possible in the frank and easy terms of family life." The minor seminary of the diocese was also attached to St Bede's and by the 1970s, when it was finally closed, some five hundred priests had received their early training at St Bede's. When Vaughan's cousin Snead-Cox wrote in 1910 more than two thousand boys had been educated there and for that year there were one hundred and eighty students, "a lasting monument" to Vaughan.

When Vaughan became Bishop of Salford the Pope allowed him to remain superior of his missionaries but he was instructed to hand over rectorship of St Joseph's College to an assistant. He offered the post to Canon Peter Benoit who had been Bishop Turner's secretary at Salford. Benoit became Vaughan's vicar and the second founder of the missionary society. He was missed at Salford where he was known by many for his kindness.

When Vaughan handed over to Benoit there were ten ordained priest members of the growing society. At first Benoit directed only the College but soon he became Vaughan's collaborator and very often acting superior of the society.

The chapel at St Joseph's College was opened on the feast of St Joseph in 1873. In April 1874 a special statue and altar to St Joseph was dedicated as the national shrine of St Joseph by Cardinal Manning.

New Missionary Projects

In the United States Vaughan began the first general chapter of his missionaries on 26th January 1875. The meeting in Baltimore produced the first body of rules for his missionary society and a structure of leadership. Vaughan was selected superior general for life. But soon communications between England and the American Province broke down. The missionaries there were committed to working exclusively among African-Americans. Then a mission was opened by the society in Madras in 1875 that began a process of subordination of the American Province. Morale plunged and threatened the continued existence of the American mission.

On 2nd November 1875 Cardinal Manning presided over the departure ceremony for the first four missionaries bound for the Telegu Mission in the Madras vicariate in India. At the end of 1876 four more were assigned. By the middle of 1878 there were twelve missionaries from Mill Hill in India. For Vaughan it was the formation of a native clergy that was a priority and he praised the founding in Nellore of St Joseph's Seminary in 1882 in two thatched huts.

In 1879 a request came from Rome to provide chaplains to the British Expeditionary Force during the second Afghan War with the hope that once the war was over Mill Hill might have a permanent mission. Four missionaries arrived in India in May 1879. When the British army was defeated at Maiwand in July 1880 hope for establishing a Catholic Mission ended. Some years later Mill Hill Missionaries would return to the Punjab and Northern Frontier.

John Aelen (later archbishop of Madras) in South India.

Another project of Vaughan's was the search for a community of nuns that would complement the society and the missionary college. This was realised when a group of four women, "zealous members of the Third Order of St Francis" who had been living in Rochdale for two years, were recommended to Vaughan. They were led by Alice Ingham. In March 1875 Alice and three of her companions travelled to Mill Hill to join the College household. The Franciscan Missionary Sisters of St Joseph was formed during their years of service. At the College they made a great sacrifice in leaving Rochdale for the dependence and silence at Mill Hill.

A Period of Loss

Herbert Vaughan's father Colonel John Vaughan and his stepmother Mary Weld Vaughan became seriously ill in Biarritz in 1880. She died of a stroke and a few weeks later on 16th December 1880, Colonel Vaughan died. On 7th January 1881 they were both buried in the vault beneath the chapel at Courtfield. Herbert succeeded to a life interest in the estate but gave up his right of inheritance, as did three other brothers who were also priests, to another brother Francis. Herbert received an annuity of one thousand pounds per year which he handed over to some of his projects.

In 1882 Herbert Vaughan lost his friend of twenty seven years, William George Ward. The funeral Mass was offered at Weston Manor on the Isle of Wight by Bishop Weathers and the homily was given by Vaughan. Vaughan thought that there were only two living men whose influence on the Catholic Church in England was greater: Manning and Newman.

The following year, 1883, there was another personal loss for Herbert Vaughan. On 18th August his brother Roger, Archbishop of Sydney, died shortly after returning to England for a rest at Ince Blundell near Great Crosby. Roger Vaughan, English and Benedictine, was often opposed by his fellow bishops and some members of the clergy in Australia which one commentator connected to the "bitterness of the religious situation that had torn England and Ireland apart."

Roger also was criticised for the kindness he extended to Mary MacKillop, the foundress of the Sisters of St Joseph of the Sacred Heart. Roger's successor refused to arrange for Vaughan's body to be brought back to Sydney. It was a very harsh incident that ended up in the newspapers. Roger Vaughan's remains were not transferred to Sydney and buried in the cathedral until 1946. The whole incident helped to strengthen Herbert Vaughan's resolve to remain indifferent to public opinion which was the mark of the final years of his life.

Vaughan experienced periodic bouts of illness during the 1880s. One symptom was insomnia. His doctor advised him to walk six miles each day. He wandered about Manchester visiting hospitals and churches. Probably as a result of his walks he discovered that the less fortunate

Catholic children of the diocese were being neglected by the Church. He became engaged in a project to care for poor Catholic children. He regretted that he had neglected caring for them in his first years as bishop but now founded the Catholic Children's Rescue Society. It became one of his lasting achievements. Manning on the other hand had struggled to care for poor children from the time of becoming Archbishop in 1865.

"The Loss of Our Children"

At Salford Vaughan became the force behind the society from the day it was founded in 1886 until he went to Westminster. He immediately applied his energy and diocesan resources to the problem. In September 1885 he asked each parish to take a census and to note the condition of any Catholic under the age of twenty one. Vaughan was touched by what he saw in his diocese; his sense of duty and fidelity to the old faith and his conscientiousness were to mark his concern for the children.

He set about rallying his diocese with a pastoral letter in 1886 titled "The Loss of Our Children." His answer was the Rescue Society. Austin Oates was appointed honorary secretary.

Vaughan continued to regret overlooking the care of children in his pastoral care even after Rescue was founded. He turned to Alice Ingham's Franciscan Missionaries of St Joseph for help. The sisters became so closely associated with Rescue that they became known as the "Rescue Sisters." In 1889 they renovated a hall at Patricroft. As early as 1888 Vaughan considered the possibility that some children might be helped to immigrate to Canada. The first small group of eight boys and five girls between the ages of six and eleven left Salford Cathedral. Between 1888 and 1908 over six hundred children immigrated to Canada.

The Irish Issue

Vaughan became involved in the Irish Question over the years and was sometimes labelled anti-Irish. His views on the political issues of his time, notably the issue of Home Rule for Ireland, were undoubtedly not those of a very large number of his fellow Catholics. His outspokenness on the issue, and the linking of Catholic interests in the Education Question with that of Home Rule, probably had more to do with it than editorial positions taken by *The Tablet*. Like Wiseman, Vaughan's views were not necessarily inspired by any antipathy to Ireland or the Irish. He attempted to distance the English Church from Irish radicalism, which would fuel the anti-Catholicism of the later Victorian era among his countrymen, and to secure the position of Catholics in England.

The political power of Catholics was related to the number of parliamentary seats they controlled and therefore the Irish, within the Union, with their parliamentary presence were a power to be reckoned with. At one point there were only four Catholic members of parliament from England and seventy two from Ireland.

Vaughan's personal view of Irish Home Rule was complicated by his advocacy of denominational education. He helped to form the Voluntary Schools Association to fight for equal government help for Board Schools and the schools run by religious bodies so that all children have free education. He continued to work for equal treatment during his years at Westminster, and finally shared in the successful passage of the Education Act of 1902.

Vaughan carried to his death the unpopularity of his opposition to Home Rule for Ireland. At the same time, unfair criticism aroused tributes to his fairness. On one occasion in 1894 it was charged that he governed the diocese "in the interests of a political party," a statement that aroused Irish priests in the archdiocese to issue a "manifesto": "That we hereby declare that under Cardinal Vaughan we have full political freedom and have frequently publically exercised it."

Bringing the Church Before the People

The original Catholic Truth Society became defunct when Herbert Vaughan became Bishop of Salford in 1872. It was re-established in the 1880s due almost entirely to the work of one person, James Britten, a convert, and in 1884 an employee in the Botanical Department of the British Museum. He was also editor of *Nature Notes* and the *Journal of Botany* and had written several books and monographs. With a small group of about a dozen people he brought out three small Catholic publications.

In 1884 a friend of the group, Wilfred Oates, invited them to meet the publishers Burns and Oates. The meeting was unsuccessful. Britten then wrote to Herbert Vaughan. He met with Vaughan at Salford and the bishop promised his support.

In November Lady Herbert welcomed the group to a meeting at her London home and it was there with Herbert Vaughan presiding that The Catholic Truth Society was formally re-established. Vaughan obtained the blessing of the Pope and helped to establish the Annual Conferences of The Catholic Truth Society. Britten wrote that Vaughan was always ready to encourage any movement which would bring the Church before the people. The first meeting was held in Westminster in October 1888. For the remainder of his life Herbert Vaughan was an active supporter of Britten's Catholic Truth Society.

Britten quoted Vaughan in an essay on the history of the society that the scattering of tracts was not a waste for "God is always sowing His grace over the world…and for every effort we make, there is an eternal reward."

Herbert Vaughan was at Salford in 1889 when he was invited by Cardinal Gibbons to attend a centenary celebration in Washington of the establishment of the hierarchy in the United States. He was unable to attend but sent his secretary Msgr Charles Gadd in his place. He also wrote a reply to Gibbons that was called "a remarkable challenge to the Cardinal of Baltimore and the American hierarchy to realise their obligations to the task of the Universal Church." John Tracey Ellis, who found the letter in archives in 1944, went on to say that the letter showed "all the fervour and courage of Vaughan as a missionary pioneer" and revealed "a most impressive continuity of missionary policy. In a deep conviction that, no matter how slender were the resources of the Catholic Church in England, nor how overwhelming the demands upon its clergy, the Church could never hope to fulfil its end if it did not generously contribute to the expansion of missionary labours in pagan countries."

Vaughan hoped that the bishops' meeting in Washington would make a mission statement. The meeting did not make one but Cardinal Gibbons remembered Vaughan's challenge. Vaughan was to be instrumental in the plan by two American priests to begin a foreign missionary seminary in 1910. It was the beginning of Maryknoll.

New Global Missions

For his own missionary society a new mission was assigned by Rome in 1879. On 14th August 1881 Thomas Jackson and five priests arrived in Kuching, Sarawak. They met three other missionaries from Mill Hill already at work. By 1885 there were seven mission stations. Sisters from Alice Ingham's community were asked to help with education. By 1891 there were sixteen Mill Hill Sisters at four stations.

In 1886 the first missionaries from Mill Hill arrived in New Zealand to work among the Maoris on North Island. Long before the arrival of Mill Hill Missionaries Marist missionaries had started Catholic communities among the Maoris. However over the years the mission was left in the hands of a few secular clergy. Vaughan could spare only two missionaries. The beginnings were unclear but led to outstanding service for many years by missionaries from Mill Hill. By 1907 there were seventeen missionaries from Mill Hill in New Zealand.

After the failed mission to Afghanistan, a suggestion was made that a new prefecture for the Mill Hill Missionaries be established in the Punjab in Northern India. In 1887 Mill Hill became responsible for Kashmir and Kafiristan which had been carved out of the diocese of Lahore. They were to be chaplains to the British army but with the possibility of missionary work in the area. Vaughan and Benoit defined three objectives for the mission. They were committed to chaplaincy work, to education at St Thomas College, Murree, and to primary evangelisation among the people of Kashmir and Kafiristan. They were never able to establish a foothold in Kafiristan and so concentrated on the northern Punjab, Kashmir, and at first, Ladakh.

Division in the USA

The mission in the United States had floundered with the departure of its leader James Noonan in 1878 to become a Jesuit. In an attempt to instil new life into the American mission the newly ordained American, John Slattery, a native New Yorker, and recently appointed rector of St Francis Xavier in Baltimore, was appointed leader. Slattery served as provincial from 13th December 1878 to 28th February 1883. He provided strong leadership and won the confidence of the Archbishop of Baltimore James Gibbons.

While in Baltimore Slattery began to lay the ground-work for what became his most controversial plan: the development of an African-American clergy. It was Slattery who alone took steps that eventually resulted in the ordination of Charles Uncles. Slattery began writing a series of articles for the *Catholic World*, the publication of Isaac Hecker's Paulists. One of his articles was titled "The Catholic Church and the Colored People." A Hecker biographer called Slattery's articles "remarkable." In 1888 he opened St Joseph's Seminary whose students attended classes at St Mary's Seminary in Baltimore. This was followed by the opening of a minor seminary, Epiphany Apostolic College.

By 1892 Mill Hill Missionaries were caring for three churches in Baltimore and missions in other American cities. There were sixteen of Vaughan's missionaries in the United States.

The first African-American to be ordained in the United States was a Mill Hill Missionary. Charles Uncles was ordained by James Gibbons in the Baltimore Cathedral on 19th December 1891. However there was to be a change in the relationship with the American Province. Those who wanted to devote their missionary life to the service of the African-Americans formed a separate society. Four, including John Slattery, chose to form a separate society. Peter Hogan, long-time archivist of the Josephites, as they came to be known in the United States, wrote that "a door closed on Mill Hill" but a door opened "for the Josephites, to grow in strength and service to the Black community in the United States."

Archbishop of Westminster

In England Vaughan had also started a minor seminary at Freshfield, a place between Liverpool and Southport. A building that had been a Protestant boarding school with six acres of land was officially opened on 11th August 1884. It remained opened until 1971. In 1890 Vaughan finalised arrangements for a small school near Roosendahl. In 1891 another Freshfield-like college was opened in the Tyrol at Brixen. Vaughan himself leased a house near the Brixen railway station for one hundred and twenty pounds.

The overall government of the missionary society remained with Vaughan until his death in 1903. Periodically there were meetings of representatives, called chapters.

One was held in 1884. They met for sixteen days "going over the work of various missionary provinces." It was made up of six nationalities representing the United States, India, Borneo and England. He wrote: "They are all one and united in the early training of Mill Hill and in one aim and one spirit."

Vaughan's mentor and friend Henry Edward Manning died on 14th January 1892. He was in his eighty fourth year. Manning was very fond of Vaughan. He recalled once their meeting in Rome in 1852 and how their "friendship and confidence have deepened from day to day." Shadows of difference existed, and correspondence supports this fact, but the friendship endured. Vaughan was staying in his own small room at Westminster, one he had used from the time Manning went to Westminster, when the Cardinal died. On his deathbed he took a small book from under his pillow and handed it to Vaughan. It was a little book in which his wife had written her prayers and meditations. "Not a day has passed since her death on which I have not prayed and meditated from this book."

Vaughan made the funeral arrangements. His lying-in-state at Carlisle Place attracted more than one hundred thousand mourners. The four miles from Brompton Oratory to the cemetery at Kensal Green were lined with crowds, mainly the London poor. His remains were later transferred to the crypt of Westminster Cathedral, built by his successor and friend of forty nine years, Herbert Vaughan.

Herbert Vaughan became Henry Edward Manning's successor. His cousin and editor of *The Tablet*, John Snead-Cox, thought that there was never any doubt who would succeed Manning. There may not have been any doubt, in Snead-Cox's view, but there was opposition. However despite Vaughan's unpopularity, at least as expressed in the secular press, Vaughan was chosen.

Herbert Vaughan was almost sixty years old, not in good health, and it was known that he had neither the taste nor the appetite for the metropolitan office. For years Manning had made it clear that he hoped Vaughan would succeed him. In addition Vaughan had a place in national life because of his family connections, an international standing as a promoter of missions, mainly due to the success of St Joseph's Missionary College and Society at Mill Hill, his achievement as Bishop of Salford for twenty years, and his representations on behalf of the English bishops. But he was aware of his own limitations especially when he had seen the faces of London's poor at Manning's funeral. He wrote to Pope Leo asking him to choose someone else. But he wrote to a friend that he had relieved his conscience by asking to be left at Salford. Whatever happened would be treated as an "indication of God's will for me." On 29th March 1892 Herbert Vaughan was appointed Archbishop of Westminster.

Westminster 1892-1903

My recollections of Herbert Vaughan during his years as Archbishop and Cardinal are those of a grand and noble figure, one that imparted unsurpassable dignity to the Church in England, the figure of a great Prince, who was also a most humble and devoted priest, as we learned (if we did not already know it) from his admirable biography.

Abbot Hunter-Blair,
Baeda, no.12, 1937

But far off, in the background, I see a great multitude of eager faces; I hear their voices like the sounds of the waves of the sea. Who are these? They are the boys and girls of our public elementary schools – they are the strength, the hope, the population of the future – they form the young democracy that is going to rule the country, to make or mar the future of Christianity in this land.

A Vaughan letter read to the 1902 CTS Conference,
encouraging a special interest in the schools

Vaughan said farewell to Salford on Easter Sunday 17th April. He said that he "had loved that cathedral and with his whole heart he had loved his people, and he had gladly worked according to his poor ability on their behalf." About the recent press reports "he felt overwhelmed with the kindness and generosity with which they had spoken of him…in terms far and away beyond anything that he could ever claim to be entitled to."

When Vaughan arrived at Westminster, the estimated Catholic population of England was 1.5 million. In Scotland there were 365,000, and, according to the 1891 census, 3,549,956 in Ireland. Westminster diocese had 253 secular and 103 religious priests, and nineteen orders of congregations of men and forty seven of women. There were 129 public churches. His pro-cathedral was Our Lady of Victories in Kensington. London had grown from a population of about one million in 1800 to the world's largest city by the end of the nineteenth century, with a population of over four million. While the City and the West End were spectacularly rich, to the east there was "an expanse of poverty and wretchedness as appalling as, and in many ways worse than, the horrors of the industrial north." Despite the terrible conditions of the poor, London continued to draw the destitute and displaced from all over Britain, Ireland, Russia and the world. On the Friday after he arrived in London Vaughan met with The Catholic Truth Society at his residence and on Tuesday he was back in Salford to help propose candidates to succeed him there.

Vaughan was officially invested as Archbishop at the Brompton Oratory Church on 16th August. Archbishop Stoner brought the Pallium from the Pope. It was the first time the symbol of the archbishop's office had been brought to England since the Reformation. *The Times* commented that the ceremony "marked an important stage in the development of a more tolerant public attitude towards Roman Catholicism." Vaughan's installation was to set the tone of his ten years in London. He was to engage in a series of controversies with the non-Catholic world, especially with the Anglicans.

Vaughan was raised to the rank of cardinal by the Pope on 16th January 1893 along with thirteen others. Vaughan's motto was *Amare et Servire*. "Love must be the root out of which service must spring up. Without love, service demanding care and self-sacrifice will never endure." Despite the impression given by his "stateliness of manner and bearing" those who knew him well found him to be a person of "infinite tenderness" and a man of the spirit.

The Building of Westminster Cathedral

Vaughan's efforts to secure recognition for the Catholic Church in Britain differed from Manning's. On Vaughan's arrival in London he announced that a cathedral was to be built for Westminster. The building of Westminster

Cathedral was to be both symbolic of his general attitude as well as an example of his administrative ability. The laying of the foundation stone took place on Saturday 29th June 1895. The building of the cathedral during the final eight years of his life was a "symbol of Catholic resurgence, a visible monument to the triumphalism of the ultramontane church." Others saw the construction as a sign that the Roman Catholic community was able at last to build well and expensively. Thanks to Vaughan's determination and financial acumen and the architectural genius of John F Bentley, the main structure would be completed by 1903.

Vaughan felt certain that the revival of the Catholic Church in England had reached a point in its development when the restoration of the life of a cathedral was a necessity. It was an opportunity to bring to completion the work begun at the restoration of the hierarchy in 1850. While critics were sceptical of Vaughan's ability to collect the enormous sums needed, he had no doubts at all. It was his confidence in God that formed the dynamics of Herbert Vaughan's life and the secret of his success.

There were delays in construction. One was a bricklayers' strike. Another was a war between Greece and Turkey which held up the transportation of columns from an ancient Thessalonian quarry; the columns were captured and held as spoils of war. In addition, a severe winter made progress on the exterior walls impossible. The architect Bentley died in 1902. At his funeral Vaughan said that he was a "poet; he saw and felt the beauty, the fancy, the harmony and meaning of artistic recreations." Another remembered him to be nervous that the domes he had designed would collapse.

The first group to enter the cathedral was a group of children of the Crusade of Rescue. They came to give Vaughan alms collected for the construction. After giving them buns and oranges he took them into the building turning half of the unfinished cathedral into a playground. When the workers reported the damage done by the children Vaughan was not annoyed: "He was content to feel that for those children their first recollection of his cathedral would be associated for ever with a happy memory."

Return to the Welsh Mission

On 6th June 1903 there was a presentation of Newman's *The Dream of Gerontius* set by Sir Edward Elgar. With the composer present it was the first time a London audience had heard the work.

He returned to the idea of re-evangelising Wales, the dream of his youth. Vaughan proposed to have the bishops agree to petition Rome to make Wales independent of England by giving it a Welsh bishop and "a chance of conversion." *The Tablet* had already published a series on "Catholicism in Wales." In the same month, September 1892, The Catholic Truth Society at its annual conference had one paper titled: "Relation to the Catholic Church in Wales."

According to Vaughan the Catholic Church had not undertaken the care of the Welsh people since the sixteenth century "in a serious, systematic and determined manner." Vaughan urged Rome to give Wales a missionary bishop of its own, a vicar apostolic. In 1895 he consecrated the new vicar apostolic, Francis Mostyn. "So curiously does God realise the desires He inspires! He does not forget them even after forty years and more!" But the vicariate existed for only three years and then became the diocese of Monevia on 12th May 1898.

The Carmelites of Notting Hill

Over the final years of his life Vaughan became a close friend of the Carmelite community at Notting Hill and its prioress Mother Mary of Jesus. When Manning died in January 1892 the nuns felt a great loss because he had "truly been a father to them" in their early years. Looking through the approximately one hundred letters written by Cardinal Vaughan in the convent archive, "there is hardly any event or decision of importance in his eleven years as Metropolitan that was not explicitly and firmly entrusted to Carmel's prayer."

The letters also give glimpses of Vaughan's own spirituality. Mother Mary's biographer writes: "How has the legend of the remote, aristocratic, 'a very great prelate indeed,' persisted so long? There was little great or palatial here; only fatherly care for the soul that trusts him and a boundless desire to further its sanctity."

In Vaughan, Mother Mary of Jesus met what her biographer calls "the inner soul of traditional English Catholicism." The others she had known were either converts or those who owed much to the spirit of Fr Faber and the London Oratory. Here she met other characteristics: "hidden springs of tenderness and piety that had produced the Jesus Psalter in days of old, with its simple love and homely phrasing, and the silent, unadorned sanctity of men like Bishop Challoner." Mother Mary of Jesus needed this insight for the work she was to embark on in founding Carmelite communities – the first in Lancashire. Before her death thirty eight Carmelite monasteries were founded, twenty eight of them still in existence when she wrote.

Catholics at Oxford and Cambridge

When Herbert Vaughan was Archbishop of Westminster he became involved in an issue that some think was unnecessary. A leading layman of the Church of England and a French Catholic, Abbe Portal, tried to initiate a discussion between Anglican and Roman Catholic theologians choosing the topic, "The Validity of the Anglican Priesthood." They hoped for a future corporate reunion of the churches. Instead it became the focus for suspicion and misrepresentation.

The validity of Anglican orders was formally rejected by Rome on 13th September 1896. Herbert Vaughan was the leading public figure of the events surrounding the papal rejection. At the same time he was representative of the feelings of many Roman Catholics in England. One commentator thought that Vaughan like many of his co-religionists was "simply ignorant" of the realities of contemporary Anglicanism. But it was Vaughan who thought that straightforwardness would win out in the future. In a letter to the Pope signed by each bishop they wrote: "When the truth shall shine much more clearly upon our beloved fellow countrymen than it does at present, it will be owing to the frank and unambiguous declarations of Catholic Doctrine and practice which your holiness has given in the face of the whole world."

One of the first major problems to confront Vaughan at Westminster was the prohibition by Propaganda Fide for Catholics to enrol at Oxford or Cambridge. For Vaughan and the bishops the question was "whether or not the Catholic aristocracy were to be given the same opportunities to acquire a higher education as were becoming increasingly available to Catholics of the middle classes." At a special meeting of the hierarchy on 4th January 1895 Vaughan proposed that the bishops petition Rome to the effect that attendance at Oxford or Cambridge be tolerated provided there were adequate spiritual safeguards. The petition was approved by the Pope and a council formed in England to implement the directive from Rome. A few months before his death Vaughan wrote to Propaganda that the permission had worked out very well, that "Catholics have done themselves great credit in both Universities."

Widening the Church Community

During Lent of 1894 Cardinal Vaughan organised a general mission for all the Catholic parishes of London. It included a census of the thirty one London missions. He was distressed by the findings during the 1894 mission. There were twenty four thousand young Catholics between thirteen and twenty one who were practically lost to the Church; "we have eighty thousand Catholics who are practically unknown to the Clergy; we have at least one million people who practise no religion and are like heathens. I am sent to all of these, to do the work of Christ for their Salvation."

He tried to reach the youth through the Catholic Social Union and the clubs the Union established. One thought that the Catholic Social Union clubs he started were one of his most important, though not so well remembered, enterprises. He continued to worry: "The work is enormous – a mission to the East End millions. How to begin! How to go on! What to say! What to do!" he wrote to Mother Mary of Jesus.

There were other groups of Catholic immigrants in his diocese besides the Irish. The large numbers of Lithuanian and Polish Catholics, and especially their children, concerned Vaughan. He started by welcoming the Sisters of the Holy Family of Nazareth to work in London, to teach catechism to the children.

He challenged the age with Town Hall Lectures, the Historical Research Society and the Catholic Missionary

Society. He wrote in February 1903 that although there were three hundred priests working in the archdiocese, there were millions outside the flock but "within our reach." Their spiritual condition was like that of the "inhabitants of China, Japan, or Central Africa." It was to these millions that he sent the "Westminster Diocesan Missionary Society of Our Lady of Compassion." A convert Anglican minister, Charles Rose Chase, was made the leader. He was succeeded by Vaughan's nephew, his brother Reginald's son and his own namesake, Herbert Vaughan. It was under Vaughan that the organisation became the Catholic Missionary Society. Despite all his good works Cardinal Vaughan felt that he had failed to accomplish more to bring people to Christ. He kept praying for light to show him how to do more.

African Missions

Over the years Vaughan continued as superior of his missionary society. He continued to remind the Church in England of the needs of the un-evangelised world outside of Great Britain.

As early as 1879 Vaughan had written about a Church in Africa not ruled by Europeans but by African Christians. "Here is a vast, unknown country, with an enormous population of intelligent human beings, having an area more than two hundred and forty times the size of England and Wales...The God who made us dependent upon those who preached the gospel of salvation to our souls has made them dependent upon us."

In 1894 Vaughan realised his dream of participating in the evangelisation of Africa. It was not done by African-Americans recruited by the Josephites in the United States, but by his missionaries from Mill Hill. They were invited to go to East Africa in 1894 to the north-eastern area of the Nyanza vicariate of the White Fathers. It became the Vicariate of the Upper Nile. Vaughan wrote from Mill Hill that he saw off a small party lead by Henry Hanlon to Uganda. They left Mill Hill on the evening of 9th May 1895 and after a long arduous journey reached Kampala in Uganda on 6th September 1895. Sisters from St Mary's Abbey, Mill Hill, led by Mother Kevin, arrived in 1902, and immediately began to care for the sick on Nsambya Hill.

Vaughan faced issues of morale, division and a lack of financial support for his Mill Hill Missionary Society. But despite problems the council that supported the Society continued to meet every six months. A meeting held in Archbishop's House, Westminster, on 16th April 1902, chaired by the Marquis of Ripon, reported that contributions for the last months of 1901 had totalled £866 2s 4d. In addition fourteen new missionaries had been sent out. There were eighty six priests and three lay brothers on the missions, twenty seven priests and eight lay brothers caring for 117 students in Europe. A place had also been opened in the South of France for sick or retired missionaries.

Mill Hill pioneers to Uganda, including Bishop Hanlon, 1895.

At a meeting near the end of 1902 the cry from mission areas was heard that despite the need for workers "We are at the end of our means! We cannot support more Fathers." At the end of the meeting it was decided that nothing should restrict the number of vocations and that God would provide an outlet for all those who offered themselves to the missions.

Crusade of Rescue

Vaughan's work on behalf of poor Catholic children did not end when he left Salford. Manning had worked tirelessly for a network of Poor Law Schools but the Catholic Homes were unable to cope with the numbers of children needing help. Vaughan appointed a commission of inquiry. One result was to have an officer attend nineteen police courts and follow up on 130 cases. Agents were then used at the courts to claim custody of Catholic children. One great problem was that there was no machinery available in the archdiocese to deal with every case of child destitution that might come before the courts. Vaughan did something to remedy this when as a result of a pastoral appeal the Crusade of Rescue was formed and joined with the older society the Homes for Destitute Catholic Children in 1901.

After his death, a small booklet gave thanks to Vaughan as "a lover of children" and acknowledged that "this beautiful side of his character" was a side that was not fully appreciated "even by his intimate friends." The title of the pamphlet was "The Children's Cardinal" by Mrs Olive Katherine Parr.

Vaughan considered the struggle on behalf of voluntary schools begun at Salford and continued at Westminster as one of the most important works of his life. Before he was installed at Westminster on 19th June 1892 he published a pastoral letter in support of the Catholic School committee. Financial support, a "question of life or death", was needed for the running of three teacher training colleges and the need to employ diocesan inspectors of education to make sure that the teaching of religion was not subordinated to the need to pass secular exams successfully.

Herbert Vaughan, though active and influential, was representing the Catholic Church, a minority school proprietor in England and Wales. He was one participant, although an important one, in an effort waged by the Church of England and others on behalf of denominational education.

At the beginning of the twentieth century it was clear that there was a need for educational reform. Vaughan held firmly that in any reforms rate aid for existing schools and those that might be built in the future would be maintained. Despite what became a terminal illness Vaughan was often in the Commons following the debate on the issue. Finally the Education Act of 1902 was passed and received the Royal assent on 18th December 1902. The general effect of the new law was to make Christian education a part of the law and constitution of England.

His cousin Snead-Cox was with Vaughan for the last time before he left Archbishop's House in 1903. They talked of the fight for schools and Vaughan returned in his thoughts to the earliest days of the struggle. There was "an exultant tone in his words as he spoke which was in odd contrast to his physical weakness" as he remembered the struggle until "the bedrock principle of equality had been reached."

A Lifetime of Service

Wilfred Ward tried to sum up Vaughan's ten years as Archbishop of Westminster in a 1910 review of Snead-Cox's biography. Many, especially Anglicans, recalled Herbert Vaughan's "flourishing the unwelcome claims of Rome in their faces" and with his "red Biretta" as a cardinal constantly offended their national feelings. Their annoyance was doubled because of his physical presence, family and social connections, and the fact that he was a prince of the Roman Church.

There were other incidents where his words caused a flood of criticism. There was a controversy of his use of the term "Roman Catholic" in a letter to Queen Victoria on her Diamond Jubilee in 1897. And on her death in 1901 about a letter he wrote from Rome to be read in all churches of his diocese where he wrote that it would not be right to perform religious services for her, rites "instituted for the souls of her own children." Snead-Cox also remembered the "bold and brazen beggar" who could not remember faces and names even of donors who had given him a great deal of money, and failed at times to recognise some of his own priests.

Despite his public mistakes, many were attracted to the very simplicity and sincerity that got him into difficulties, and seemed to support the opinion of some that he was a zealous, but blundering romantic. To his friends Vaughan had many lovable qualities "but sincerity was at the root of them all. Certainly few men have had friends more loyal and devoted than he had, and very few have known so well how to make others share in their own high and holy enthusiasms." When he died in 1903, he left many of them a legacy of love inspired by his kindness and loyalty. He also left his Church a cathedral and numerous institutions founded over a lifetime of service.

The Death of Herbert Cardinal Vaughan

Herbert Vaughan's health began to deteriorate in November 1897. While travelling through Essex on "a kind of missionary tour" he had a sharp pain in his heart and found it difficult to breathe. It was similar he said to an attack he experienced forty years earlier at St Edmund's, Ware. He returned to Westminster in April 1898 depressed in mind and body. In spite of his illness Vaughan continued to travel and work. During November 1898 he rested at Mill Hill and then returned to Westminster. The following year his general health gradually weakened despite his retreats in Wales, his periods of rest in Derbyshire and St Joseph's College, Mill Hill.

In April 1902 he went to the Visitation Convent in Harrow. He continued to work on a manuscript he had started years before of conferences on the apostolic life of the priest that was later published as *The Young Priest*. The other manuscript he completed in his final months was a translation of a devotional book in Italian titled *Humility of Heart*. Vaughan added an introduction to the English version titled "Thoughts and Sentiments on Humility."

In June 1902 he suddenly collapsed again and was forced to give up his work and take a complete rest. His doctor ordered him out of the country to Germany for treatment. In August he returned to England "weaker than when he had left and knowing that the end was near." On 19th March, St Joseph's Day, his condition worsened and he received the last sacraments. On 25th March he left Archbishop's House for the last time and travelled to St Joseph's College, Mill Hill, to await death. On Thursday 18th June he felt much weaker and made a public profession of faith in the chapel, wheeled there by his nurse.

Vaughan's Jesuit spiritual director, Daniel Considine, visited him on the day of his death. He wrote later that he found Herbert Vaughan in a deep depression. He looked into the darkness and thought, "What if Faith after all were but a dream, and all its gracious truths mere pious imaginings?" The horror, the cruelty of the temptation, lay in its whisper that "nothing was true, all beliefs were false together, there was no God, no hereafter." After being seized by such "bewilderment and terror" calm finally returned and "he knew that God was with him even if hidden behind a veil."

The next day Considine learned that Herbert Vaughan had died the previous night, 19th June 1903. At about 11:30 p.m. the Cardinal had grown worse. He whispered that he had had a bad attack. He remained calm in his chair praying, "Jesus, Mary, Joseph." It was the Feast of the Sacred Heart.

On Saturday 20th June "The Death of Cardinal Vaughan" was placarded in London and the next day a letter was read throughout the diocese describing his final days and death. In the Sunday evening twilight the great west door of Vaughan's and Bentley's unfinished cathedral was thrown open for the first solemn religious ceremony to be held within its walls. That night the coffin containing his body was brought from Mill Hill. Beginning on Monday the cathedral was open to the public and people began to file in. It was Vaughan's express wish that not "a single unnecessary sixpence should be spent upon his funeral" and it was faithfully observed in the "severest simplicity and plainness." The solemn requiem Mass was held on Thursday at 11 a.m.

Amare et Servire

The Times wrote that:

> The late Cardinal was the third of the eminent ecclesiastics of the Roman Church who claimed to exercise direct spiritual jurisdiction, territorially allotted, over members of the Church in this country. The half century which has elapsed since the Ecclesiastical Titles Act, 1851, has witnessed an enormous change in the attitude of the English people towards the Roman Catholic Church, and in his measure each of the three archbishops contributed largely to that result.

On the Thursday morning the cathedral was already crowded before the Mass. Bishop Stanley, Vaughan's auxiliary, offered the Mass. Bishop John Cuthbert Hedley of Newport gave the homily. Cardinal Logue, Primate of Ireland, gave the final blessing. The coffin remained until the next morning when it was removed to St Joseph's College, Mill Hill. The hearse arrived at the College at 8 a.m. and the body was carried to the chapel where a Mass began at 9:30 a.m.

Herbert Vaughan's brother Bernard gave the panegyric. He told the story of his brother's life. He thought the secret of "your Father's spiritual success in life and death" could be found in his motto, "*Amare et Servire*, to love and to serve." He seemed to put "before his eyes, simply, tersely…contemplation and action, of prayer and labour, which it is the business of every apostle to make his own if he is to become an efficient instrument in the hands of Jesus Christ for the salvation of souls."

After the final blessing the students carried his body to the small cemetery where he was to be buried below a large crucifix he had brought from the Tyrol many years before. In 2005 Cardinal Vaughan's remains were removed from the Calvary cemetery and carried from St Joseph's College to Westminster Cathedral where they were welcomed by Bishop George Stack and reinterred in the chapel of St Thomas of Canterbury.

A Nation for Catholics

A note in Vaughan's final instructions to his executors stated: "I beg pardon for all the scandal and bad example and for much neglect of God. But I die in peace in the arms of the Blessed Virgin Mary, my Mother – professing all that the Church professes and teaches."

To know the mind of Herbert Vaughan one might learn much from the prayers he left behind. In a prayer book of his missionaries he wrote:

> I offer Him all, I ask to be allowed to surrender every fibre, He alone being the Master of every string and note belonging to me. He may take away my health and capacity, send me failure and public dishonour – dry up my soul like the dust, if only He will support me, and let me love and serve Him.

Any weaknesses in Vaughan's work can often be traced to his temperament and health problems and a consequent inability to take on the everyday tasks of his office as a seminarian, Church leader or founder. He had a grand vision of what might be accomplished by hard work and prayer and in this he was enthusiastic; it was a contagious enthusiasm. He questioned the bright and the wise, and recorded their ideas and experiences. To enable his projects to function he gathered around him loyal and hardworking people, clergy and lay, who shared his vision or wished they could.

He had a vision of the Church as the Rock of St Peter, providing stability in a time of revolution, the papacy standing firm for unity after three hundred years of reformation in his country. As unpalatable as his views about authority and modern philosophy and liberalism may seem today, they were part of his vision.

One of his grandest projects was the missionary training college and society he founded at Mill Hill. The expanding British Empire, seen on the coloured maps of his day, beckoned and challenged him to action.

He saw his cathedral not only as a place for the liturgy but as a centre that was alive, the head and heart of the Roman Catholic community in Britain. His lifelong habit of regular prayer enabled him to accomplish much with his skills despite his limitations.

The Times on Friday 1st December 1995 reported that Queen Elizabeth II had attended Vespers at Westminster Cathedral on St Andrew's Day to mark the cathedral's centenary celebrations. It was held to mark the one hundredth anniversary of this "Christian-Byzantine style building, which Cardinal Vaughan began to construct in 1895. But the service is more likely to be remembered for a different reason. By her presence in the cathedral yesterday, Her Majesty the Queen became the first British monarch since the Elizabethan Settlement to attend a Roman Catholic Service in this country."

Cardinal Hume welcomed the Queen as she sat below the altar. "The presence of Your Majesty in this cathedral is for us a further affirmation of the place that we Catholics have in the nation."

The Humanity of Vaughan

It took years of study before finally writing about Herbert Vaughan's extraordinary life and achievements. And yet despite the accumulation of information I did not experience a personal connection until one day I recognised him in a photograph with a small group of Rescue children on their way to adoption in Canada. There he was in profile, wearing a biretta, looking sad and uncomfortable, yet trying to show his concern for the most vulnerable in his care. In that moment he became for me more human. The story of Rescue grew from his personal regret that he had failed as a bishop. He had neglected to care for the poor Catholic children in his diocese. It was only in 1884 that he became aware of the condition of those children: orphans, street children, juvenile criminals and others. Many were in workhouses and were being "lost to the faith by the thousands," he wrote.

The Catholic Children's Rescue Society became a project that was a reminder of his failure and at the same time a public achievement. The case of poor and neglected children, one of the most serious social conditions of the times, stirred him to action. Not only did he publically apologise for his failure to address the problem sooner but he did extraordinary acts of penance. More than once he was found on the doorstep of the Mill Hill Sisters in Patricroft putting on his boots. He had walked from the train station barefoot, as a personal act of reparation for his failure to act on behalf of the poor children sooner. His efforts continued and expanded at Westminster. In 1899 the Crusade of Rescue was founded to care for every destitute Catholic child in London.

The failure had also brought about a change in Vaughan, a tenderness that was often missed by others. It was in 1901 that the first public group entered the unfinished cathedral. They were children of the Crusade of Rescue who brought Vaughan the alms they had collected for the construction. They turned the interior into a playground. When the workers reported the damage they had done Vaughan was not worried but rather was pleased that the children would have a happy memory to carry away of the cathedral. His fight to care for poor children revealed the depths of his disappointment with himself and a more gentle side to his personality. Katherine Parr's booklet *The Children's Cardinal* revealed this gentler side of Vaughan's character that even his closest friends did not know.

The Gift of Humility

In December 1894 Herbert Vaughan was ashamed to discover that he had been given a nickname for the way he was known to rush through liturgical ceremonies. Cardinal Goodier wrote years later that pictures of the

cardinal showing him relaxed, "a figure of calm dignity, give the wrong impression. He could never be still in mind or body…so swiftly did he perform religious ceremonies – little train bearers had to run to keep pace with him – that many people thought him irreverent and called him the 'scarlet runner.'"

Being made aware of this was a great shock to Vaughan. He was so ashamed that for some time afterwards he broke down in tears when offering Mass. He wrote to apologise to the clergy of Salford diocese that during his years as bishop he had performed certain ceremonies and administered the sacrament of Confirmation "with such haste and hurry as to deserve the censure of scandalous irreverence." He followed with a public apology to the priests of Westminster at a synod meeting. It was an experience that "nearly crushed Vaughan's spirit."

A story that revealed a more attractive side of Vaughan's character was told by William Samuel Lilly, a Cambridge convert and writer, who knew Vaughan for many years, visited him in Salford and received him into his own home. In 1892 Lilly was invited to address an annual meeting of Catholics in Birmingham called the Reunion. He chose as the topic for his speech the "Temporal Power of the Pope." He spoke cautiously for an hour from notes about, at the time, such "delicate a subject." Some were dissatisfied with his talk and wrote in *The Tablet* "week after week" complaining about Lilly and his views.

Vaughan, who was owner of *The Tablet*, at the time was moving from Salford to Westminster and "probably did not notice the attacks" on Lilly until a mutual friend mentioned it to him. Years later Lilly uncovered the note Vaughan had written to him. "I have read with great regret a paragraph in the Tablet in which you and the Temporal Power are again brought in," Vaughan wrote, promising to "take good care that this matter shall drop. I write this hurried line to express to you my good will and my earnest hope that we may work together for many years to come. God bless you."

Lilly reproduced the letter not only because it recalled pleasant memories but because it was in his experience "extremely characteristic of the writer" to show such kindliness.

"A Prince of the Church"

Another gentle message from Vaughan was quoted in a life of the Anglican Bishop of Manchester, James Fraser. On the death of Fraser in 1885 Vaughan wrote to his widow from St Bede's College where he lived in a small apartment: "I can never forget the nobility, the directness, and simplicity of your husband's character, and the sympathetic charm which played like sunlight on his countenance. The universal tribute of admiration must indeed be a great consolation to you."

At Westminster Cardinal Vaughan became a good friend to the Carmelite community of sisters and their prioress Mother Mary of Jesus, at Notting Hill. Their archive includes approximately one hundred letters of Herbert Vaughan. His first visit did not go well for the sisters but his second, in September 1892, revealed another side of Vaughan. He gave a short talk "which opened out a new aspect of his personality and rejoiced the Prioress' soul." How had "the legend of the remote, aristocratic… great prelate persisted so long" Mother Mary's biographer wrote. In his letters there is "little of the palatial here; only fatherly care for the soul that trusts him and a boundless desire to further its sanctity." In Vaughan, Mother Mary had met someone from the heart of traditional English Catholicism with all the hidden tenderness and piety of men like Bishop Challoner.

Bishop John Campling, of Cameroon and Uganda, was a student for three years at St Joseph's College. At one point he looked after visitors and had opportunity to observe Cardinal Vaughan on many occasions. Campling was ordained on 3 March 1903, shortly before Vaughan's death. He wrote that the "cardinal was a handsome man, tall and noble of bearing, in fact he seemed a perfect haughty aristocrat to those who knew him not. I know how his shoes, robes and clothes were patched up and his clerical hat a disgrace. I found him, as all who really knew him agree, kind, gentle, really humble, a perfect gentleman, a deeply spiritual priest and a distinguished Prince of the Church."

Bishop Hedley of Newport spoke at a memorial Mass for Vaughan in the Courtfield chapel on 8th July. He urged his listeners to remember Herbert Vaughan's pastoral letters.

Nothing would do adequate justice to Vaughan's qualities of mind and heart as a complete collection of his writings. For thirty years he had never omitted, like a watchman on the walls of Jerusalem, to lift up his voice whenever there was a need of information, of united counsel, of courage, or of sacrifice. Let his friends and clergy of this country never forget him.

Further Reading

A full and thorough account of Herbert Vaughan's life is provided in *Cardinal Herbert Vaughan – A Legacy of Love and Service*, Robert O'Neil, M.H.M., 2016 (Updated Paperback Edition), Herder & Herder, The Crossroad Publishing Company.